Recipe for Disaster

Recipe for Disaster
Poems by Pamela Miller

Mayapple Press 2003

Published by   MAYAPPLE PRESS
                PO Box 5473
                Saginaw, MI 48603-0473
                www.mayapplepress.com

ISBN 0-932412-19-X

Pamela Miller can be contacted at *pmiller@enteract.com*

This book was designed and typeset by Judith Kerman in Calisto MT
with titles in Poor Richard

Cover art by Janet Bloch *www.janetbloch.womanmade.net/gallery.html*

Author photo by Richard Chwedyk

Some of these poems (sometimes in earlier versions) originally
appeared in: *Chicago Poetry Dot Net, Clutch, Free Lunch, Hair Trigger, Krax,
The MacGuffin, Moon Journal, Piedmont Literary Review, Poetalk, Primavera,
Pudding, Rambunctious Review, Seams, Seven-Oh-Eight, S.L.U.G.fest Ltd.,
Spout, Strong Coffee, Tomorrow Magazine* and *Zuzu's Petals Quarterly Online.*

Poems in this book also appeared in the following anthologies:
Dangerous Dames (11th Hour Productions, Chicago, 1998), *Freedom's Just
Another Word* (Feminist Writers Guild/Outrider Press, Crete, IL, 1998),
Animals Don't Knock! Tails from the Pet Shop (11th Hour Productions,
1999), *Feathers, Fins and Fur* (Outrider Press, 1999), *Daughter of Danger-
ous Dames* (11th Hour Productions, 2000), *A Kiss Is Still a Kiss* (Outrider
Press, 2001), *Inhabiting the Body* (Moon Journal Press, Arlington
Heights, IL, 2002) and *Take Two, They're Small* (Outrider Press, 2002).

"On Turning Fifty and Feeling Goddamn Good About It" was first
published in the calendar *Her Mark 2002* (Woman Made Gallery,
Chicago, 2001).

"Resignation Letter to the Boss from Hell" was originally published as
a limited edition broadside by Outrider Press.

This book is for my father,
Merton H. Miller,
1990 Nobel Laureate in Economics,
who taught me to always leave 'em laughing

Contents

Marie Writes a Letter to Her Husband Just Before She
    Finally Leaves the Womanizing Jerk   13

Excerpts from a Surrealist Resume   15

J.'s Anatomy   16

The Secret of a Lasting Marriage   17

Gigantic Frogs Will Come from Fire   18

Leo Kagan, His Downstairs Neighbor the Stockbroker,
    and the Arts in the Big City   20

Fish Story   24

Spring Hits Chicago Like a Sock in the Jaw   25

Marilyn Monroe at the Gates of Heaven   26

Resignation Letter to the Boss from Hell   27

What Makes a Man a Man   29

Women Waking Up in the Morning   31

Running in Circles   32

Mail from Home   33

Marcella's Rubber Hair   34

Living at the Movies 2: Hollywood Salutes
    "The Celebration of Women in Films"   35

From "The Body at Fifty"   37
    1. The Body in Motion
    2. Body Functions
    3. The Body Reinvented

My Part of Town   40

The Good Life   42

Roger's Spring Fever Love Song   43

International Survey Finds Men Are Unnecessary   44

Valentine   45

Lullaby   46

Recipes for the Perfect Man   47
    1. Smooth-Talking Man
    2. Mystery Man
    3. Four Million Dollar Man

Trouble   52

Bashō's Frog Jumps into the Pond for the 538th Time   53

Mutability   54

The Dream I Had on the Last Night of the
    Year Before You Died   55

Ode to Joy   56

Love Story   57

Invoking the Muse   58

Recipe for Disaster   59

On Turning Fifty and Feeling Goddamn
    Good About It   61

"Woman is not ward nor slave nor toy nor curio."
—Gwendolyn Brooks, "Chicago, 2999"

Marie Writes a Letter to Her Husband Just Before She Finally Leaves the Womanizing Jerk

I wish you a plague of scorpions,
scuttling, brown and sinister as
all my years with you:
scorpions in your coffee,
your hairpiece, your bank account,
nothing but names of scorpion species
in your throbbing
little black book.

May you be plagued with failures:
promotion after promotion
flapping away like uncatchable crows,
your lucky streak snapped like a
broken jaw,
the life of Job wallpapered
all over yours. And as for your grandiose
long lush manhood,
towering and proud as the Chrysler Building,
may it sink, sink, sink like the Spanish Armada,
never to sail again!

I will you a plague of vaginas,
angry ones. No, not the kind
with the tired old teeth,
but vaginas that march around in your head,
clomping and stomping their furious lips;
that cancan up and down
in your chest, kicking away at
your heart. Vaginas that
sprout on your face like pimples,
cunts that encrust on your butt like barnacles,

one for each mistress and
thousands for me,
shouting me on as I bolt to daylight,
oh million fierce mouths of my morning,
laughing your name down to Hell.

Excerpts from a Surrealist Resume

for Penelope and Franklin Rosemont

CAREER OBJECTIVE
An endless midnight traipse through a parliament of swans
upon the River of Light.

SUMMARY OF QUALIFICATIONS
Award-winning spangled pomegranate. Delicatessen strangler.
Expert at stealing the moon's three cufflinks. Clever little salmon
of God.

EDUCATION
B.F.A. Sapphire Licking, University of the Break of Dawn.

PROFESSIONAL ACCOMPLISHMENTS
Amphora, Gnats & Libido, Inc. (1995-Present)
* Created alphabets of lightning.
* Improved a small apocalypse.
* Designed flamenco limericks on Heaven's pink back porch.
* Developed a snake dance of spontaneous human
  combustion.
* Expedited blueprints of disease.
* Planned and implemented swirling collisions of
  copacetic brains.

REFERENCES
Available in hoarfrost.

SALARY REQUIREMENTS
Infinities of broccoli. The gleaming tooth of glory.
A closetful of brand new souls.

J.'s Anatomy

His hair unfurls like grand opera.
His eyes are the ocean where the
Giant Squid cavorts.
His chin is the end of the world
as we know it. His mouth,
that monster, guzzles Loch Ness.

His shoulders are two far-flung festivals.
His arms swoop up to rattle
the constellations like chandeliers.
His chest is a forest of
rococo oaks; his hands,
snazzy spiders that prowl my breasts.

His belly is a big bass fiddle
strummed by the Duke of Earl.
His thighs drawl and murmur
and sing me to sleep all night.
And his knees kneel down
and his back sprouts wings
and his lungs scream bloody hallelujah!
His hips are the Grand Prix de Monaco
and I win! I win! I win!

The Secret of a Lasting Marriage

for Mert and Kathie
on their twenty-fifth anniversary

It's such a shy, uncluttered secret, actually,
small enough to write on a
hothouse grape. It's the
dazzling goddess of Compromise,
with Rita Hayworth hair,
shuffling round the house in a
ratty old bathrobe
which the brawny, yodeling god of Romance
washes without complaint. It's
learning to give and take, like a trombone.
It's simply that marriage is a
two-way street—the Champs-Elysées
lined with flags and flowers,
down which you and your spouse march towards each other
at this weirdly glacial speed
while all of life's beanballs
bonk down on your heads:
custard pies and rubber checks,
golden bowls and mastectomies,
in sickness and in health, Napoleon and Josephine,
Fred and Ethel, for better and for worse.
And when, after marching for twenty-five years,
you finally meet at the moonlit Rond-Point,
up pops your gorgeous retirement home
like some great soufflé of love. And you
glide through the front door
arm in arm,
draw the drapes and dim the lamps,
and at last, by the light of
your shimmering silver,
as always, you do.
You do.

Gigantic Frogs Will Come from Fire

"'The Last Frog' examines the unexplained phenomenon
of mass deaths of frogs all over the planet. While reports
of grotesquely deformed frogs in Minnesota lakes
grab headlines, researchers are baffled by the sudden
disappearances of scores of frog species, even some that
live in pristine areas."
—Ad for a 1996 *National Geographic* TV special

On the day the new millennium unfurled its flags
gigantic frogs arose from fire,
straddled the globe like squiggly pagodas,
baby-faced and furious,
to rescue Earth from the world.

Spurred by the healing hug of their legs,
the earth grew back its
hacked-off forests,
the blackened rivers skimmed off their toxins
like small boys spitting out squash. Nudged
by their towering wise-eyed heads,
the ozone layer reknit itself,
exquisite and proud as a wedding dress,
an invincible star-spangled bandage.

The deformed frogs from the factory towns
rose from their Lazarus lakes to be cured,
their hideous pinwheels of extra legs
cauterized by deft tongues of flame.

On the day before the Frog King rested,
all the world's cities turned to
placid ponds. Billions of tadpoles
surged up from their depths,
cavorted and jigged like "Jabberwocky."
Humankind faded away

like a rash. Except for
one virgin in her boat of blonde hair,
who had hidden a frog
from dissection class doom,
chosen as the one pure breeding bride
for the brave new Buddha-shaped prince of fire
in his blazing green garden of peace.

Leo Kagan, His Downstairs Neighbor the Stockbroker, and the Arts in the Big City

1.

Who is it
that puts these strange green brochures
in my mailbox every day?
> *TONIGHT! At midnight*
> *Leo Kagan will draw rings around the moon.*
> *The public is cordially invited.*
I find this so annoying,
climbing the stairs to my apartment
one at a time:
I have films from France and Hong Kong
to go to, I have gorgeous brochures
from people who want to sell me
motorcycles and cars. I have successful
friends with black hair
all over town. I find this
so annoying. It has nothing to do with me.

2.

The strange man from upstairs
spends the whole damn day shuffling across his floor.
Knocks at my apartment
every night, with every excuse in the book
to make talk:
  "May I borrow an English muffin?"
Loud and moving slowly
in my living room,
wearing down my rugs, endlessly talking
  "May I examine your Life *magazine?"*
he stares at my television
and gives me these weird warnings,
pointing
out my big dirty window
in his too-stiff green suit
like old wallpaper, like counterfeit money.

3.

This is not your house, Leo Kagan!
This chair was not put here
for you to shuffle by,
this rug wasn't made for you
to walk on in a frog-ugly suit.
This rug was made for women in suede skirts,
Leo Kagan, who sit
in this chair, who stretch out and
touch this rug with
just one toe,
then tilt back their incredible heads
so carefully, Leo Kagan,
as if crossing a bridge.

4.

At midnight the strange man from upstairs
goes out to meet
his public. Tunneling deep
into the suburbs,
a subway car all to himself,
he arranges himself in the window like a work of art,
his arms in beautiful angles. But
nobody's watching,
no one even sees his great silhouette
like some Japanese cartoon.
At the end of the line
there's just one man on
the platform and one man on the train.
He leans out the window
and yells politely across the tracks:
> *"SIR!*
> *This is the end of the line.*
> *Now if you and I will take the train together*
> *back downtown,*
> *I promise you a performance!*
> *A performance!"*

Fish Story

At night I release all the fish
from my hair. Shore-leaved from me,
they grow big as zeppelins,
swim down the airwaves
of a dozen all-night oldies stations,
head out over the city
leaving trails of smoke and pearls.
They sail off to places
my sisters would never approve of,
wrap their gills around long white men
like squirming strands of spaghetti,
send a message to the man in the octopus tuxedo
to report to my bedroom pronto.
The moment his tentacles
glide down my gown,
the whole room fills with seawater. Later
I trim his beard
on the carpet which has turned to a coastline,
shiver to one last scherzo
of suckers down my spine. When he goes
he leaves his love knob
for me to scrimshaw in the morning
as fish after fish after homecoming fish
pokes her joyous face through the walls.

Spring Hits Chicago Like a Sock in the Jaw

Suddenly, streets warm as neon; we scamper down them stiffly
like Prince Charles. Birds *shreeeep*ing their heads off: the Battling
Bickersons in every tree. Babies wiggling in windows. Jellybeans
stuck to shoes. Men on sidewalks selling silly bumper stickers.
Some aren't bad: *WE HAVE NOTHING TO LOSE BUT OUR
PANTS.* Dogs become aristocrats, promenading the town.
Mushrooms pop up on lawns with cute little *boing!* sounds.
Newspapers revert to stream of consciousness. Poets lean out
windows and take off their clothes. Some do not succeed.
The mayor is constantly on television, his squash-shaped face,
vaguely military, filling the screen. He smiles at us, waves, eats
potato chips with his no-good son. But we ignore them, because
it's spring. Time to go to the lakefront and eat things on sticks,
to pluck up blades of grass and pickle them in jars! Time to sit in
the baseball stadium and watch the sky revolve, watch the days
grow long and layered, like candy bars.

Marilyn Monroe at the Gates of Heaven

Lord, here I come
wearing nothing but my ballgown
of a body. At the end
of it all, it's just me.
It's me, it's me, it's Sugar! Tired
as a Chinese mountain
of tap-dancing down Niagara Falls
over and over and over and over,
spluttering-wet and naked
to the world. Spread out your
great clean hands for me,
like a bathtub, a towel,
a nightie. Cuddle me up and hide me,
like a long white mink
eclipse. Storm off the set with me
tucked in your arms. Be my
barrel. Be a blonde's best friend.

Resignation Letter to the Boss from Hell

*To K.K.—My mama didn't raise me
to work for a jerk.*

Get out of my life
you inky shoe,
you pencil-snap duke of bad cabbage!

Who do you think you are
you swaggering germ,
you hairy spittoon,
you slug-shiny dollop of hooey!

You ain't nothin' but a
chamber pot fez,
a fruitcake in a bat-wing toupee.
Go stick it in your ear
you tuxedo of fleas,
you feculent chasm of cancer!

I'm free at last
you tantrum of splat,
you lichen-faced fop,
you bucket of gunk with
intestinal handles,
you greasy smear of ratatouille
on the dazzling white smile of life!

I'll see you in Hell
you cathedral of slime,
with your yaws chandelier
and your fungus cologne
and your gangrene tattoos
and your spider-leg teeth,
oh you sheep-dip chow mein that I
spit out spluttering
because it tastes like death in striped pants!

Find yourself a new sucker,
you mechanized yam.
Eat wasps. Grow an udder.
Drive your car off the cliff
of your cheesiness.
And may crazed hippopotami
spit on your wife:
Spa-tooh! Spa-tooh! SPA-TOOOOEY!!!

What Makes a Man a Man

for Richard

I tried to make a man out of
diamonds and quartz,
with a big rectangular ruby for a heart
and a mirrorball head that shot light all around,
but the jewels clouded over
or kept falling off
or smelling like eight-month-old green cottage cheese,
so I broke him apart
and buried him in the ground
and that was the nasty end of *that*.

Then I tried to build a man out of telescopes
and put my eye to his heart
to see what I could see,
but all I could spy through that cold glass dot
was his face up some skirt in Amsterdam,
and a pair of smirking breasts in a Bangkok hotel,
and some Martian's coy eyelash
purring down his cheek,
so I broke him apart
and buried him in the ground,
where he could keep his damn eyes to himself.

So I finally made a man
out of junkyard parts
and bound them together with Christmas lights,
then inserted a heart like a red silk frog,
and a big old brain the size of a rump roast,
and read him throbbing Armenian love poems
for thirty days and nights. And he
dug us a nest and he snuggled us in

and he tangoed inside me
    oh helium! handclaps!
painted frescoes inside me
    kazoo! orchid! bonfire!
and we burrowed on down to
the center of the earth—
oh plunge-and-soar hot honeymoon,
sweet ruckus of getting it right!

Women Waking Up in the Morning

for Arlene Zide

Nancy wakes up
like The Crazy World of Arthur Brown,
smoke pouring forth from her pillow
and *FIRE IN HER BRAIN!*

Julie wakes up
with squids in her hair,
wings on her back,
and a sparkling drop of spit in her eye.

Jo-Ann wakes up
and goes to her job at José's Limbo Lounge
wearing nothing but
three well-placed conch shells.

Karen wakes up every morning
and slides off the edge of the world.

LaTanya wakes up
like Krakatoa erupting,
like an endless Sylvester-and-Tweety cartoon,
an opera of pots boiling over.

Mary Catherine wakes up
in a moon-cold sweat
and discovers her fingers
are missing.

And I, born in Athena's right ear,
fifty years old in my
nightgown of poems,
these days I wake up, up, up, up, up,
forever rapturously rising.

Running in Circles

All night long
the sky has been changing colors in circles,
revolving like a squad car light
    black   white   gold
    black   white   gold

All these years
you've been running from me in such swaggering circles,
giving me the slip
like a greased Fred Astaire,
tattooing the globe with your
frantic footprints
as you hunt out new hiding places
with a paleontologist's glee
    Cleveland   Paris   Mars
    Cuba   Tibet   death

Night after night
I dream this same Zoetrope dream of you,
circular slapstick cartoon
that spins faster and faster
and will never stop:
    I race to you   kiss you   miss
    Forever
    race   kiss   miss

Mail from Home

First of all,
the usual letter from Uncle Philip. This time
he claims to have patented
a zeppelin made of noodles. As always
I fold his letter up quickly
and throw it away. From my mother
there's another ridiculously long letter
on her strange old Great Gildersleeve stationery.
She goes on and on
about a one-legged Latvian movie star
who was at somebody's wedding.
It takes me more than an hour to read this.
Plus my cousin Arnold
has sent me his screenplay
for a *Hamlet* set in the Stone Age
and Uncle Malcolm the architect
has enclosed blueprints
of the brain-shaped church he's designing. Someone
has sent me a postcard
of a Matisse nude
with an obscene word stamped on it. On the back
it says "You old pirate!"
and there are three dirty limericks. Of course,
my twelve-year-old cousin Wendy
has sent her latest poems,
which make me cry a little
because they are all written on a
really beautiful light blue paper bag
and are about Japan.

Marcella's Rubber Hair

Marcella in her beauty:
her elastic band hair
bouncy and delicious about her shoulders.
God! It stretches
and snaps. Children are always pulling at it.
Marcella, indulgent
with ivory waist, tiny breasts.
Her hair as raincoat,
snowshield, prodigious umbrella.
A lover wanders in it for a while.
When she's tired of him
she slingshots him into the next county.
At midnight, a whispery sound,
a lit lamp:
with a snippet of hair
she's erasing his love letters.

Living at the Movies 2: Hollywood Salutes "The Celebration of Women in Films"

Woman-Bait
Woman Chases Man
Woman Eater
Woman Hunt
Woman in a Dressing Gown
Woman in Bondage
A Woman in Flames
Woman in Hiding
The Woman in Question
The Woman in Red
A Woman Is a Woman
Woman Obsessed
A Woman of Affairs
A Woman of Paris
Woman on the Run
A Woman Rebels
A Woman's Devotion
A Woman's Face
A Woman's Secret
A Woman's Vengeance
The Woman They Almost Lynched
Woman Times Seven
A Woman Under the Influence
Woman Wanted
Women Are Like That
Women Are Weak
Women in Cages
Women in Limbo
Women in Love
Women of Devil's Island
Women on the Verge of a Nervous Breakdown
Women's Penitentiary or The Big Doll House

The She-Beast
She Couldn't Say No
She Couldn't Take It
She Dances Alone
She-Devil
She Done Him Wrong
She Drives Me Crazy
She Gets Her Man
She Knows Too Much
She Learned About Sailors
She'll Be Sweet
She'll Have to Go
She Married Her Boss
She Played with Fire
She's a Sweetheart
She's Back on Broadway
She's Dressed to Kill
She's Gotta Have It
She's Having a Baby
She's in the Army Now
She's Out of Control
She's Working Her Way Through College
She Waits
We're still waiting.

from The Body at Fifty

1. The Body in Motion

The Body looks in the mirror
and notes that she is no longer
shaped like a pin
but more like the grand prize winner
in a contest for bizarrely shaped vegetables.
So she boots the mirror out the window
and prepares for her morning jog.
The Body dons volcano-print panties
and a T-shirt made only of
sheer girlish innocence
and chugs off down the avenue,
her xylophone bones all a-clatter.
Butterflies alight on the Body's head
like passengers on the Queen Mary.
Shoestores and cinemas give way to wheatfields
that wave her endlessly on.
Sunset drips down the back of her neck
but the Body keeps moving,
on tyrannosaur legs,
in Atalanta's sandals,
on impossibly hot-wired electric skis
that blaze grooves of fire in her wake.
Now wings sprout glibly from the Body's feet
like hopped-up time-lapse crocuses
barreling into March
as the Body takes off and soars skyward,
a gleaming Concorde of flesh,
surging through the stratosphere
like a spear hurled at God's front door.
Oh, the Body at fifty resembles a squash
grown in the shape of Mount Rushmore,
but see how gracefully
she threads her way through life,
like a single strand of angel hair
slipping through the keyholes of the stars.

2. Body Functions

The Body at fifty
still has lots and lots of guts

and more menstrual blood than Del Monte has ketchup,
and great roiling vats of estrogen
that overflow like the Johnstown Flood,
and a long, smooth, silky vagina
like an elbow-length glove filled with honey. But
some dried-up dragon

with a pumice tongue
keeps rasping at the pages of her calendar,
keeps sending her postcards
of empty vessels,
of lush plums collapsing into prunes. So the Body

grows herself a new fur coat
and long red underwear that
itches like fire,
to prepare herself for the inexorable ice,
the thirsty winter winds.

3. The Body Reinvented

How odd to wake up at fifty
in this body of loose boards
and tumbling bricks

with its hair like chipped paint
and its bleary breasts
like the eyes of exhausted yaks,
its back like a suitcase
full of iron nightgowns,
and its boarded-up womb—
a museum awash with ghosts.

But a body still wearing
that sly mauve dress
and dancing shoes frantic as castanets

that refuse to scrape off
or be hauled away
or dissolved in the fumes of time's turpentine
or hacked to chop suey by the surgeon's knife
    oh, won't you come dance with this body
with its songs that keep sprouting
like a million brash buds
and its face of unquenchable
five-year-old's joy
hardening into a diamond.

My Part of Town

The street where I live is all hot pink
and I mean *HOT!* Our
imported Turkish trees,
their wondrous, huge fruit
like fourteen-karat beach balls, dazzling at noon...
The people on my block are so
fabulously intense
pepper plants spring up from
their footsteps when they walk.

You, on the other hand, live on a street
where all is whalish gray,
or the color of exhausted tarpaulins,
or of Thousand Island dressing
gone very, very bad. Which is why
I love to bring you presents
from my boisterous part of town:
lawn chairs made of fruit,
life-size neon dinosaurs,
the flags of a hundred nations to
festoon your front porch—
I just want to help brighten things up.

When night splashes down on
my part of town,
our houses come alive like
taste buds. The roofs pop off,
flap like wings and sail away,
fireworks shoot from every room,
punch the sky so full of holes
that miles and miles away
the Statue of Liberty,
the stoneheads on Mount Rushmore
crane their necks to see. To
see us...what?

What dances do we do
around these swimming pools filled with opals?
What mythical beasts do we
breed and barbecue
in these backyards luxurious as
Cleopatra's thighs?

Come visit us tonight.
You can read our deep dark diaries:
At midnight we turn into comets
and spill our blazing secrets down the sky.

The Good Life

Nuggets of gold dipped in
French chocolate.
Chocolates dipped in gold.

Mink coats
sprayed with twenty karat gold
then rolled in diamonds.

First course at the banquet:
a black velvet pig stuffed with
caviar and pearls.

A check for
a million bucks
drizzled with platinum.

Rolls-Royces
doused with Cointreau and ignited.
(For the ultimate kick,
try to *drive* it flaming!)

Photocopy machines of
the very rich:
sheets of beaten gold
in the paper tray.

Caviar big as baseballs.
Emeralds big as airports.
A solid gold tombstone and
no one in your grave
and you whisk it all away with you
to Paradise.

Roger's Spring Fever Love Song

Margaret's wild forelock—
flying Irish hair! Shoes
of ice cream, feet of ice cream!
She sent me some ringlets
and I hid them away,
like stars in a box, like
vows underground!

Red leg of love
and white leg of love!
Strong legs of Margaret, dance on me!
I'll build you a house in Monaco,
a cone-shaped house with
windows that breathe,
with rings around it like Saturn!

I'll become a tycoon
of spaghetti sauce,
recipes etched in gold
on my brain! I'll give you
an orchid every day,
sprouting on the screen
of a miniature TV!

Oh Margaret with shapes
of airports in your hair,
I'll name frogs and galaxies after you!
And I'll love you down to
your very core,
to your skeleton, that string of pearls!
To your atoms, you tower of swirling jewels!
Oh Margaret, let me
climb you to Heaven!

International Survey Finds
Men Are Unnecessary

"TENNESSEE WOMAN MARRIES A FROG!
Memphis bank teller Karen Moller
couldn't find herself a Prince Charming
so she stopped trying and married
a frog named Georg."
—*Weekly World News*

Tennessee woman marries a frog

Montreal woman marries a cheese

Swedish woman marries a cello

Tokyo woman marries a wall

Paris woman marries the Seine

Ugandan woman marries Mars

Thai woman marries a small brave word

Chicago woman marries herself

Valentine

With thanks to Thax Douglas
for the first line

The sea is a spy in my washing machine
and each year my moiré birthday cake
grows a thicker layer of spongy paranoia.
But just put me in a
honking big bed with you,
and I become the goddess of
hammers and nails,
of butter and hair,
of love becalmed in a rowboat
made of muscles and
mother-of-pearl. But how
can I make love to you
like the inscrutable scissors that I am
when the bed keeps turning
to a toucan at your touch,
when confetti shoots out of
the toasters of your eyes
and makes my heart whir
like an x-ray? My head
shrinks down to the size of a grape
as my heart balloons to a zeppelin
of red lamé stretched tight as a high C,
huge as the island of Zanzibar.
And with you at the rudder
and me in flames,
we'll fly forever in and out
of Saturn's tricky shadow,
for you are the god of
the lavish spoon of love
stirring the itchy neutrons of desire.

Lullaby

for Rich and the guys

When frogs fly
The dinosaurs will return.
My love, close your eyes.

The dinosaurs will return,
Tiptoeing on giant feet,
While you and the bears and the
Sky sleep.

Dream about zeppelins big as France,
About fudge that beeps
And muffins that bounce.

Frogs will zoom through the clouds
As the President stares.
Squids will do the cha-cha everywhere.

Close your eyes like a hedgehog
Scrunched in a ball.
Frogs will fly
When the first star falls.

Recipes for the Perfect Man

1. Smooth-Talking Man

Also known as "The Miller Special." A delicious,
extremely slippery man, always in demand.

Preheat oven to 350 degrees.
Prepare the following custard:
    4 ounces ingratiating Frenchman
    1 cup Million Dollar Club salesman
    1 cup Luciano Pavarotti, firmly packed
    1 teaspoon Mephistopheles
Cook and stir in a double boiler over plenty of
hot water.

Sift before measuring:
    2 cups erotic poetry
Blend with:
    a 10-gallon hatful of honey
    3 barrels molasses

Beat well:
    1 wild, wild whirl around the
    dance floor
Add 1 forked tongue gradually. Blend until
thrilling. Beat in, one at a time:
    365 lies

Add the poetry-and-molasses mixture to the
lies-and-dance-floor mixture
in 3 parts, alternating with thirds of:
    1 quart extra-slick motor oil
    1 cup goose grease
    2 tablespoons mercury
    1 tube Brylcreem
Stir the batter until smooth-talking after each addition.
Stir in the Frenchman custard.

Whip until soft:
    1 patent leather tuxedo
Fold it lightly into the batter.

Bake in greased pan for about 25 minutes.
Cover, when cool, with:
    your body

2. Mystery Man

This curious combination of ingredients
makes a surprisingly good man. But why
shouldn't it? The deep secret is peach wine,
which is, after all, a sweet.

Preheat oven to 98.6 degrees.
Sift before measuring:
    2 cups your long-lost prom date
Resift with:
    ½ teaspoon lion tamer
    1 teaspoon zeppelin repairman
    ½ teaspoon each Byron and Shelley
    2 teaspoons corporate raider

Sift:
    1 cup stupendous sumo wrestler,
    great placid Taj Mahal of flesh
Cream until soft:
    ½ cup Frederick the Great
Add the sifted sumo gradually
and cream these ingredients well. Stir the
prom date mixture into the sumo mixture,
alternating with thirds of:
    1 10½-ounce can cream of mad scientist soup

Fold in:
    1 cup rock star named Artie Farty
    with stained-glass hair down his back
Add:
    5 drops dejected diplomat
    from a country of sad silver lakes

Bake in greased pan for about 45 minutes.
When cool, get him drunk on:
    peach wine

3. Four Million Dollar Man

This is the old-time One-Two-Three-Four Man,
slightly modernized.

Preheat oven to 950 degrees.
Sift before measuring:
    2 cups boring old boy next door
Resift with:
    1 gold lamé Italian suit
    5 Rolls-Royces
    The whole damn bank at Monte Carlo
    1 mile-long solid platinum yacht
    with a hold full of Krugerrands

Sift:
    1 diamond big as Disneyland,
    finely diced
Cream until soft:
    1 cocaine empire
Add the diamond pieces gradually. Cream these ingredients
until very rich indeed.

Beat in, one at a time:
    4 million dollars
Add:
    4 humongous bodyguards
    like Mount Rushmore with legs

Add the boy-next-door mixture to the cocaine mixture
in 4 parts, alternating with fourths of:
    1 night together on a long, spectacular
    strand of moonlit beach
    1 prenuptial agreement
    sparkling in the stars
Stir until luxurious after each addition.
Fold in lightly:
    4 condoms

Bake in greased pan for 35 minutes.
Remove man, increase heat to the max
and set the world on fire.

Trouble

I've got the whole wicked world
between my earrings,
smoke my cigarettes nasty-style—
lit end *in*. And what about
those big red fangs
you plucked out of me in your
dream last night?
Danny, do you know what trouble is?

I'm the queen of the walking wounders.
And you're so exquisitely bruiseable,
a banana that can't find his skin.
Instead of counting sheep
you chase them
up and down minefields in your dreams all night
while I give your heart a hotfoot,
smash your heart's windows—
Danny, don't you know what trouble is?

Even with platform shoes on stilts
you're out of your depth.
I'm all ten kingdoms of Chinese Hell,
the slashdance round and round your heart,
I'm the wheel of life and death
broken down in a ditch
in the Dust Bowl. Danny, Danny
close your eyes and lie still.
You'll find out soon enough
what trouble is.

Basho's Frog Jumps into the Pond for the 538th Time

Suddenly the pond
has a frog in its eye.
Splouch!

Mutability

You're not a man, Dave, you're a
committee—a collection of
twelve different water sprites,
their outlines all wiggly,
constantly bringing me gifts
from that hideous Center for
Unpleasant Surprises:
    toenails
    tarantula earrings
    brackish aphrodisiacs from Haiti
    with toads floating inside.

You flicker and change like a barnyard:
dogs chasing chickens, then
goats chasing dogs. You're a North Star
that splits like an amoeba,
a road map that keeps sliding
off the page. All I really want

is one uncluttered man,
simple as a vowel,
one anchored-down face to
kiss, to *"yes,"*
dependable and firm, like peanut butter. Tonight,
in bed with six of you—
    set after set of
    wings unfurling inside me—

I suddenly know I'd do anything,
anything, even finger a voodoo flute
under a fuzzy full moon,
if I could just distill you down
to your one exquisite essence: a man
made of brandy,
useful and sublime.

The Dream I Had on the Last Night of the Year Before You Died

You were leaning against a wall
smoking a cigar
made of bones.

You walked down the street
and each building you passed
collapsed like a
worn-out marriage.

I kissed you and you tasted like
Black Plague cake,
like drinking poisoned wine
in the Catacombs.

And I woke up and shook you
and my hand went
right through
and kept going, past the
edge of the world.

Ode to Joy

*With thanks to the late, great Paul Carroll
for the first line*

I feel so goddamn good today
that when the smelly old catfish of gloom
tries to hang above my head like an ugly '50s lamp,
I punch it away like Muhammad Ali,
shouting: "THIS OLD GIRL JUST WANTS TO BE HAPPY
AND WHEN I'M THROUGH WITH YOU
YOU'RE GONNA LOOK CRAPPY!"

And when the orchestra gets huffy
and refuses to play
my Concerto for Nose Flute and Singing Frog
on the grounds that
it's, well, *preposterous,*
a gigantic hand descends from the sky
and smears them all with peanut butter.

And when my man comes to me
with his shirt on fire
and spreads himself before me like a picnic,
then takes from the basket
his midlife crisis,
all squirmy and whiny and covered with gack,

I just ride on my ostrich and
swing on my swing,
dance naked on top of the Trump Taj Mahal,
and then wad him up into a basketball
and stretch him out into a slide trombone
and whip him up into a banana split,
then drizzle it with rum
and enjoy.

Love Story

She was the girl
with enormous eyes and enormous toes,
with the frog motel right next to her heart
and a baby giraffe curled up in her head
where the poetry should be.

He was the man
with the pointed head and the basketball butt,
the great flat feet like sourdough loaves
and a single miniature angel wing
sprouting from the back of his neck.

How twitchy their trysts
though they fit together like Sam and Dave,
circling each other like
yogurt-covered atoms,
like timid spies on stilts.

How solemn their wedding
atop the hood of a tiny French car
as their seventeen friends stood by in the park
holding tinfoil sculptures of God.

How dazzling their kids,
like tall white cacti with flaming hair,
future designers of space travel blimps
and great gleaming trees of world peace.
How lithe their young bodies,
dancing and leaping in hydrogen leotards,
how rowdy their bodies,
doing the dragon-dive into their prom clothes,
how perfect their bodies,
perfect as pocketknives,
covered all over with breathtaking poems
that look strangely like
wondrous wings.

Invoking the Muse

for Susan Wooldridge

Oh Muse, in your poem-white robe of light,
clutching a wreath of storms
to your breast,
your stern right arm pointing moonward,

bring me words
that clatter like hearts,
that tango on stilts
of fire. Transform
my small shy sonata of breath
to a swooping tornado of stars.

Recipe for Disaster

Take one flat-out no-good man
with conniving fingers like
French cigarettes. Add
one rusty little box of a town,
one great big bottle of nitroactive gin,
a truckload of broken hearts like
old rotten turnips,
and my truculent teenage radio
that *never* plays "Stand by Your Man."

    Stir, set aside, and
    allow to fester.

Meanwhile, in separate bowl, mix well:
two cups extra-sharp fishbones;
seven long switchblades, opened;
three quarts psychochloric acid;
one tankful of gas;
the head of that floozy he dumped me for,
an ounce of blood from each woman he's hurt,
and one skeleton key.

    Fold in no-good man mixture.
    Stir so violently
    every tree in town falls down.

Slide the whole nasty mess
into a microwave-unsafe casserole.
Garnish with putrid pimientos
and sprinkle with me, me, me!
Sprinkle me so thick and swarming
I blot out the whole damn sun.

    Microwave on High for
    three long years.
    Go on—push the button. I dare you.

Serves two:
that skirt-swizzling, swoondoggling, slimslamming,
twelve-timing no-good rotten skunk.
And me.

On Turning Fifty and Feeling Goddamn Good About It

for Liz Marino, forty-five
and ticking

A woman's place
is in her bones—
not tending the gaudy newsstand of flesh,
nor spraying red paint
on the fading walls
in the chichi boutique of her hair.

A woman's place is in her skin,
which she should wear like
Ruth Bader Ginzburg's robes,
sweeping majestically up the stairs of her life
like a peacock tail of stars
to that glittering spree of a party
in the ballroom on the fiftieth floor.

A woman's place is
in her time—not facing backwards
like an unspent coin, but
blazing down its streets in a silver Corvette
made of sheer chandelier-swinging joy,
tangoing slyly through its
airports and zoos
in Minerva's tiara of fire,
shaking time's hand and caressing its groin
and getting it drunk in her giddy penthouse,
winking one coy eye at her
two-faced future:
the incredible shrinking dance floor
and the wildly widening light.

About the Author

Chicago poet Pamela Miller's literary career began in her sixth grade English class, where she won first prize in a short story contest for her piece about a man-crazy female gorilla named Lizzie who liked to wear earrings, hats and lipstick. (Lizzie also had an obsessive urge to sit on caterpillars—perhaps Ms. Miller's earliest known use of an erotic image.) She has since gone on to win such honors as three Illinois Arts Council Literary Awards for Poetry, first prize in both the 1998 and 1999 Feminist Writers Guild poetry contests, first prize in the Jo-Anne Hirshfield Poetry Awards and three Pushcart Prize nominations. Her work has appeared in many literary magazines and anthologies, including *The Paris Review, Free Lunch, Primavera, Pudding, Poets On:, Naming the Daytime Moon: Stories and Poems by Chicago Women* and *Women and Death.* She has published two previous books of poetry, *Fast Little Shoes* (Erie Street Press, 1986) and *Mysterious Coleslaw* (Ridgeway Press, 1993). Her performance poetry piece, "How to Handle a No-Good Man," has been presented at venues coast to coast, including The Knitting Factory in New York City, N.A.M.E. Gallery in Chicago and the Keane's 3300 Club reading series in San Francisco. Ms. Miller lives on Chicago's Far North Side with her husband, science fiction writer Richard Chwedyk, and 700 frogs.

Other books from Mayapple Press

Gerry Lafemina, *Zarathustra in Love,* 2001
    Paper, 44 pp., $8.50 plus $2.50 s&h,
    ISBN 0-932412-18-1
Judith Kerman and Don Riggs, eds.,
Uncommonplaces: Poems of the Fantastic, 2000
    Paper, 148 pp., $15.00 plus $2.50 s&h,
    ISBN 0-932412-17-3
Poems by leading s.f. and fantasy authors, including Brian Aldiss,
Joe Haldeman, Jeanne Larsen, David Lunde, Patrick O'Leary,
Rick Wilber, & Jane Yolen
Helen Ruggieri, *Glimmer Girls,* 1999
    Paper, 40 pp., $8.00 plus $2 s&h,
    ISBN 0-932412-16-5
Zack Rogow, *The Selfsame Planet,* 1999
    Paper, 40 pp., $7.50 plus $2 s&h,
    ISBN 0-932412-15-7
Larry Levy, *I Would Stay Forever If I Could,* 1999
    Paper, 36 pp., $6.50 plus $2 s&h,
    ISBN 0-932412-14-9
Skip Renker, *Sifting the Visible,* 1998
    Paper, 36 pp., $6.50 plus $2 s&h,
    ISBN 0-932412-13-0
Hugh Fox, *Strata,* 1998
    Paper, 28 pp., $5.50 plus $2 s&h,
    ISBN 0-932412-12-2
John Palen, *Staying Intact,* 1997
    Paper, 28 pp., $6 plus $2 s&h,
    ISBN 0-932412-11-4
 Judith McCombs, *Territories, Here & Elsewhere,* 1996
    Paper, 28 pp.,$6 plus $2 s&h,
    ISBN 0-932412-10-6
Kip Zegers, *The American Floor,* 1996
    Paper, 24 pp., $6 plus $2 s&h,
    ISBN 0-932412-09-2
Al Hellus, *a vision of corrected history with breakfast,* 1995
    Paper, 24 pp., $5 plus $2 s&h,
    ISBN 0-932412-08-4

David Lunde, *Blues for Port City,* 1995
    Paper, 24 pp., $5 plus $2 s&h,
    ISBN 0-932412-07-8
Evelyn Wexler, *Occupied Territory,* 1994
    Paper, 80 pp., $10 plus $2 s&h,
    ISBN 0-932412-06-8
Evelyn Wexler, *The Geisha House,* 1992
    Paper, 24 pp., $5.50 plus $2 s&h,
    ISBN 0-932412-05-X
Judith Minty, *Letters to my Daughters,* 1981
    Paper, 24 pp., $5 plus $2 s&h,
    ISBN 0-932412-04-3
Toni Ortner-Zimmerman,
As If Anything Could Grow Back Perfect, 1979
    Paper, 16 pp. ,$5 plus $2 s&h,
    ISBN 0-932412-02-5

Also available through Mayapple Press:

Judith Kerman, *Plane Surfaces/Plano de Incidencia,* 2002
Bilingual, translations by Johnny Durán
    Paper, $15 plus $2 s&h, CCLEH,
    ISBN 999-34-0-312-1
Dulce María Loynaz, *La Carta de Amor al Rey Tut-Ank-Amen/The
Love Letter to King Tutankhamen,* 2002
Bilingual, translation by Judith Kerman, limited edition, signed
    Paper, $15 plus $2 s&h, CCLEH
    ISBN 999-34-0-315-6
Judith Kerman, *Mothering & Dream of Rain,* 1996
    Paper, $12 plus $2 s&h, Ridgeway Press,
    ISBN 1-56439-062-4
Judith Kerman, *3 Marbles,* 1999
    Paper, 88 pp., $7 plus $2 s&h, Cranberry Tree,
    ISBN 0-9684218-1-4
Judith Kerman, *Driving for Yellow Cab,* 1985
    Paper, 16 pp., $5 plus $2 s&h, Tout Press,
    ISBN 0-932412-04-1

Sample poems and the latest information for all Mayapple Press
publications are available online at **www.mayapplepress.com**